THE BODY YOU'RE IN

Phoebe Wagner is a poet, theatre-maker and performer from London. She studied at Rose Bruford College on the European Theatre Arts course and was part of the Roundhouse Poetry Collective in 2014-15. She is part of *Living House Theatre*. This is her first pamphlet.

The Body You're In

Published by Bad Betty Press in 2019
www.badbettypress.com

Cover design by Amy Acre

Printed and bound in the United Kingdom

A CIP record of this book is available from the British Library.

ISBN: 978-1-913268-01-5

The Body You're in

BAD BETTY PRESS

Seen through a mirror, I viewed my body as another.

– Ocean Vuong

The Body You're In

To my Mum

Contents

Pins and Needles

I am reading but her sleeping breath

makes all the words become
leaning heads. *My shoulder remembers*
girls heavy with their light
loudly rattling on my shoulder.

She is starry flecks cutting the film.

Lips loosening in kitchens, a dare that is the truth.
Her face in zoom, pores and skin, lifting to the camera.
Subtitles tell me her lips were fragile and soft.

She is pointillist.

Cut to tangled legs
hidden feet
in between screaming *so close—*
when is this going to happen?

When she wakes, I am stamping
to get the blood flowing again.

Bi-ral

Mum asked if I felt like my life was Eastenders because I cried a lot
and I remember answering yes.
Thinking *no*.

It was there to make the insertion easy, comfortable and clean.

He told me he doesn't understand bisexuals because
Why should you have more choice?

When you put a tampon in water, it expands and leaves bits of
cotton floating in you.

Thinking *Pink gin makes me feel like a woman.*
Thinking *I want to go to Peckham and Netflix with her again.*
Thinking *I fancy you because it's unusual.*

The fibres stick to the vaginal wall.

When she shows me where to go,
I am a haze.
She shows me where the satin is,
where hot rain can pour.
The motion of my hands chugs to a halt,

thinking *Independent and scientific studies have proven that it's because
you roll up your jeans.
I am a cotton-rayon blend.
I only pretend to like women.*

Nudes are Flowers for Men

When you arrange your bouquet, choose his favourites.
Or if you don't know what type he likes,
at least go for the classics.

Make sure to create clear shadows with your textured body:
creases, arches and bulbs. Ignore any itches.
Try to photosynthesise your cheekbones in the light.
Say to him *I got you these.*
It's nothing.

His stone will begin to break
and it will be as if he is shifting out of a seed.
He will peer into the light,
a buttercup lifting to a neck as he says
they're my favourite.

He might go back inside,
get a vase and run the tap.
His hands gently
peeling plastic and paper. He might
ruffle them and become
wind pollinating his sentiments.

And when he's done
he will close you and place you in his pocket.
Dead and pressed amongst the others.

PUBLIC

make public bleed
make public sing and kill
make public our saviour
      lonely
homogeneous public
wholesome and easily digestible

      call public to ask its opinion
      expect public to respond with a clear answer
      make public wait for their post to arrive
      public opens with their many fingers whilst
      not public uses a knife
      not public sits at a desk
      and sketches plans for public
      can't see the blueprint
      only accessible in private

      when it's walking alone in the dark
      the possibility of attack
      makes it hard to find private when public is always public

public shaves in private
that's the only time public is private
the transformation is a shower stream shattering the skin
when public is finally allowed to see
all its hairs go down the plug hole
the only one to see
the sketches become a scribbled mess entering the bloodstream of the city
these private moments can only be colossal
bigger than the fraction of time they take up

must fill the quota   must become symbol   must be the sign

the leftover drain rats
our new-found skin glow

Woman Dressed in a Vagina Costume

She points to the squidgy globe above her head
I know as Firmness.

She points to another hole
I remember as the place my hand was guided towards.
Her hand saying this is where the ocean pours into a river.
The myth of squirting,
that all women if named will swell.

She points to her ribs
two sausages on the outside—
her hands point in downward strokes.
Hairless pillow, pink.

Mine are the question
is the carpet the same colour as the curtains.
I know them as Flaps.

A trap door for a bedtime ritual I can't look at.
Here she stands, a velvet mass on a woman's body.
I have been tasked to name each part of her.
She is dancing for the countdown
what is this
                    and this
                                    and this...

Container

You were all fingers
pressed into me
all where you could put yourself
and where best my body fit
you were all how much
can I fit
and how much out of 10
am I going to be
how many people have I been with
are you a good dancer
what's your best move
how many t-shirts can you pile
me in the back corner
unfolding
how random this is
how many can I fit into her?
can I fit. Fit
girl
that day you wore those jeans
I'd never clocked before
These were your answers
Questions sleep with you
I tell you I have a vibrator
I don't want you to know
your teeth
watching me nearly
xx

A Panic Attack

Thought is (a trigger)
a specific word (a torrent)
growing. They think you're (insert word of choice)
losing (memory as it is happening).
Concrete (feet, a drunk-carpet)
chest (a footrest),
ghost eyes (see-through).
The brain (goosebumps)
is a bruise (a waiting-magnet)
wanting to (hit pole—run tap—sharp snag)
boil (purple).
Too small to notice (bruise too big to ignore),
(how did that get there?)
bleeding (no blood).
Her body tries to become (object)
millisecond pulses (attention-seeking calculated)
in public (they're in another room).

2AM: (a girl) woman has just thrown her arm at a bus pole three
(four) times.

The bedroom silence (the rumble before the tube explodes)
wants a hug (leave me alone)
with all the other times this has happened.

Goo Goo

When I tell you his name,
it will be telling how you try to say it.
What colour is this name?
Does your mouth tighten?

It is pronounced
as if some letters have vanished.
Surprise.

You might try to say it
carefully fixing the eyes to the mouth
like a baby would.

You might give up
and rename them their country.

The name is hung up silks
spinning into a tight coil,
arms spread, tumbling
and stopping in mid-air.

It rises and rumbles
whistles, drops and throws itself out of the cave.

For you, it might feel clogged up,
burying itself between the mucus.
Bare feet on primary school gym mats.

When I say it,
I will remember trying the sounds
of a language we could both speak,
the English crawling out.

Raul

If I came out folded neatly into rolls of olive skin,
a small island of dark brown hair,
Mum would have named me *Raul*.

Raul would have eaten chicken and pollo at the same time.
Mi madre dice *No puedes tener chocolate si no lo comes.*
A father says *Come on, eat up!*

I am struggling to speak without something to translate me.
Abuela watched mixed colours spin amongst the water.
They became my Abuela's arms and mine,
the red bled on an olive Raul.

My Abuela's S's scrambled together more and more,
I came to Spain to finally learn to speak
pero no puedo decir lo que quiero decir.
I am not the Wagner that my Dad calls me.

A sewing machine punctured and sewed my mother together.
It is not her fault that she prefers names
that end in 'e', they sound friendlier,
not the wide mouth of her name Almu-THENA.
It is not her fault red falls from my head.

Abuela knew I was the devil when I came out like that.
That all of Spain had bled out of me.

Shame Bingo

It was never about you	It wasn't personal	Not meant to offend	You are always apologising		Finding a way to frame yourself as the victim	An outcry	You didn't mean it	You were fine and pretending you weren't
You are your own paperweight		Hungover	Badly timed	Time is managing you	You never proved yourself	You had control over your actions		You rushed the deadline
Overstepped the mark	Are coming down	It has taken all that was left of you		Cost too much	Your parents gave that way to you	Your relatives are too far to even pin down where that came from	A gene	The dog ate

Suffocated by the amount you always had in you	A talent of yours from a young age	You're worth more	Don't deserve	Asked for it		It is a child you bore	Begged for	It happened unexpectedly
Washing your hair	You booked a holiday for 6 months	Discovered the block button	It was always growing	Multiplying	Too stuck to get out of bed	You pried it out of its tin	Too embarrassing a haircut to leave the house	Let it grey your teeth
It came to you in a dream		The siren just a tad too far to stretch	Alarmed	Overwhelmed by the amount of news	You're just too small or the equivalent in other size ranges		An answer will come	It and you are porous

Not Him

We do not have the same knees.
The same hair.
His would have been knocking out space for themselves.
My knees apologise.
My hair envies
what it could have been.
If we met, he
might say things I wouldn't understand
because my brain is sorry.
I might cry because I would see myself
somewhere in there, a microscopic
blip in a chromosome
but I wouldn't quite
be able to speak to *the other me.*
I would only make small talk. Promise
to drop him an email
but I never will because he is
parallel.
Running alongside me
in the other men
who are boys who enjoy
not fitting in their overgrown bodies.
I could only imagine
how he befriends
himself.

The Care Plan

~~Likes to be outside with the mud and leaves and collect this in Mum's car.~~

~~Loves to collect bottle tops.~~

~~Wakes up at night and runs the taps.~~

~~Floods the house because it feels like the sea.~~

~~Is regularly in hospital.~~

~~Is non-verbal.~~

~~Favourite colour to speak is 'gree'.~~

~~Is responding well to being lead by hand to safe spaces around the school.~~

~~Points to the fire escapes as a ritual.~~

~~Needs 2 adults to help stay in class.~~

~~Likes to lie on the floor to feel the comfort of the underfloor heating.~~

~~Will always try to get onto the trampoline even when playtime is over.~~

~~Is scared of water but every swimming lesson is getting deeper and deeper into the pool.~~

Needs a lot of repetition.

This acts as armbands.

Is learning to sign 'I want more'.

Can run around the hall for hours playing chase.

Asks if it's okay? Wants to make sure it's okay.

Needs headphones to mute the stimulation of everything around them.

Finds calm in the hiding letters and numbers, will show you by tracing them in the mist.

Is 12 with a reading age of 15 but struggles to focus for more than 1 sentence.

Can calculate 17 x 426 in their head in seconds.

Mirrors my every movement very carefully matching the way I cross my arms.

Loves cuddles.

Loves nursery songs.

Prefers to sit on the grass and watch their friends at playtime.

Loves the sound of emergency vehicles.

Is learning how to say 'I played on the scooters with my friends'.

Is going to be a chef.

Is overwhelmed by the classroom.

Is an incredible swimmer.

Is going to be the highest scoring rider on Deliveroo.

Is going to bring thousands to their shows.

Is going to feel the wind on their face as they cycle to their mum's on their own for the first time.

Can remember every stop on every bus in South East London.

Can get so anxious that they bite and scratch.

Is in charge of picking up the laptops from every class on a Friday.

These children will gain adequate funding to achieve the above.

Speaking to Myself

A well covered path: the trees, sun pushing through holes made by the branches. I can hear my mum's breathing. She hears it as screeching. Out here, the folds in her throat are purring. She needs a bench and it appears. We sit and she says *the bench is sinking*. I say *do you hear yourself*, pointing out the trickle, a dying river running beside us. She says *I think I'm depressed* and I say *I know, same*. I can hear myself—*how are you going to make yourself feel better? What can you try?* Wondering when my therapist will find the holes we have made for each other. The silent crowd of trees become my ribs arched over this table trying to write a finished conclusion for you. Something you can underline and say *that's it. That's what will get me out.*

Acknowledgements

Thank you to the poets and artists in my community who are paving the way. Thanks to everyone who read this at various stages in the writing process and gave me their feedback, support and encouragement.

Thanks to the editors of *Thiiird* Magazine for including early versions of 'Container', 'Raul' and 'Not Him' in Issue #2 Femme.

My gratitude and love go out to Amy and Jake who gave me the opportunity to do this and have made this such a nourishing experience.

Thank you to my friends and family who I love dearly.

Other titles by Bad Betty Press

Solomon's World
Jake Wild Hall

Unremember
Joel Auterson

In My Arms
Setareh Ebrahimi

The Story Is
Kate B Hall

The Dizziness Of Freedom
Edited by Amy Acre
and Jake Wild Hall

I'm Shocked
Iris Colomb

Ode to Laura Smith
Aischa Daughtery

The Pale Fox
Katie Metcalfe

TIGER
Rebecca Tamás

The Death of a Clown
Tom Bland

While I Yet Live
Gboyega Odubanjo

Raft
Anne Gill

She Too Is a Sailor
Antonia Jade King

Blank
Jake Wild Hall

And They Are Covered in Gold Light
Amy Acre

Alter Egos
Edited by Amy Acre
and Jake Wild Hall

Forthcoming:
No Weakeners
Tim Wells

Lightning Source UK Ltd.
Milton Keynes UK
UKHW010843240620
365448UK00001B/47